Color testing page

this page intentionally left blank

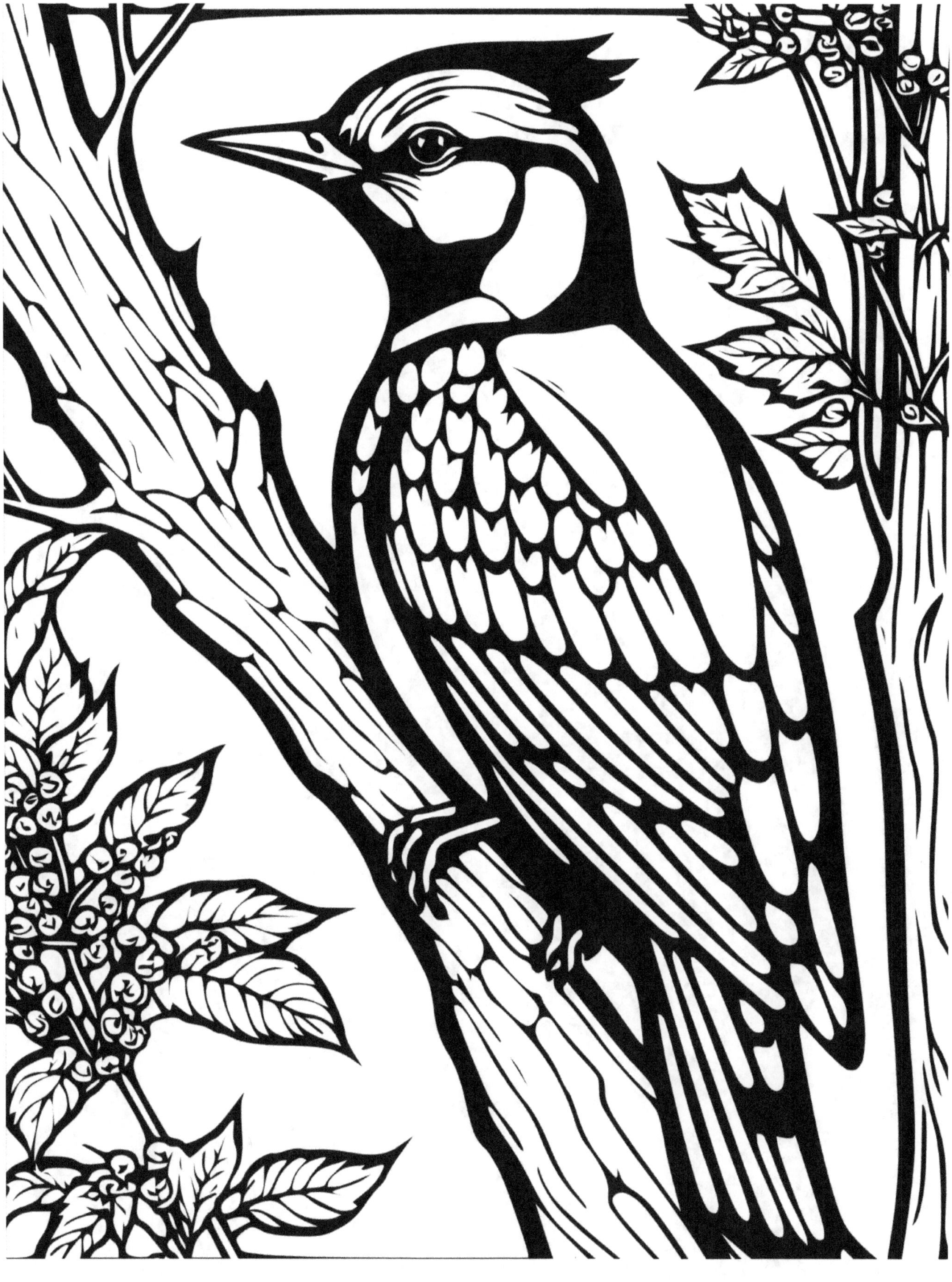

this page intentionally left blank

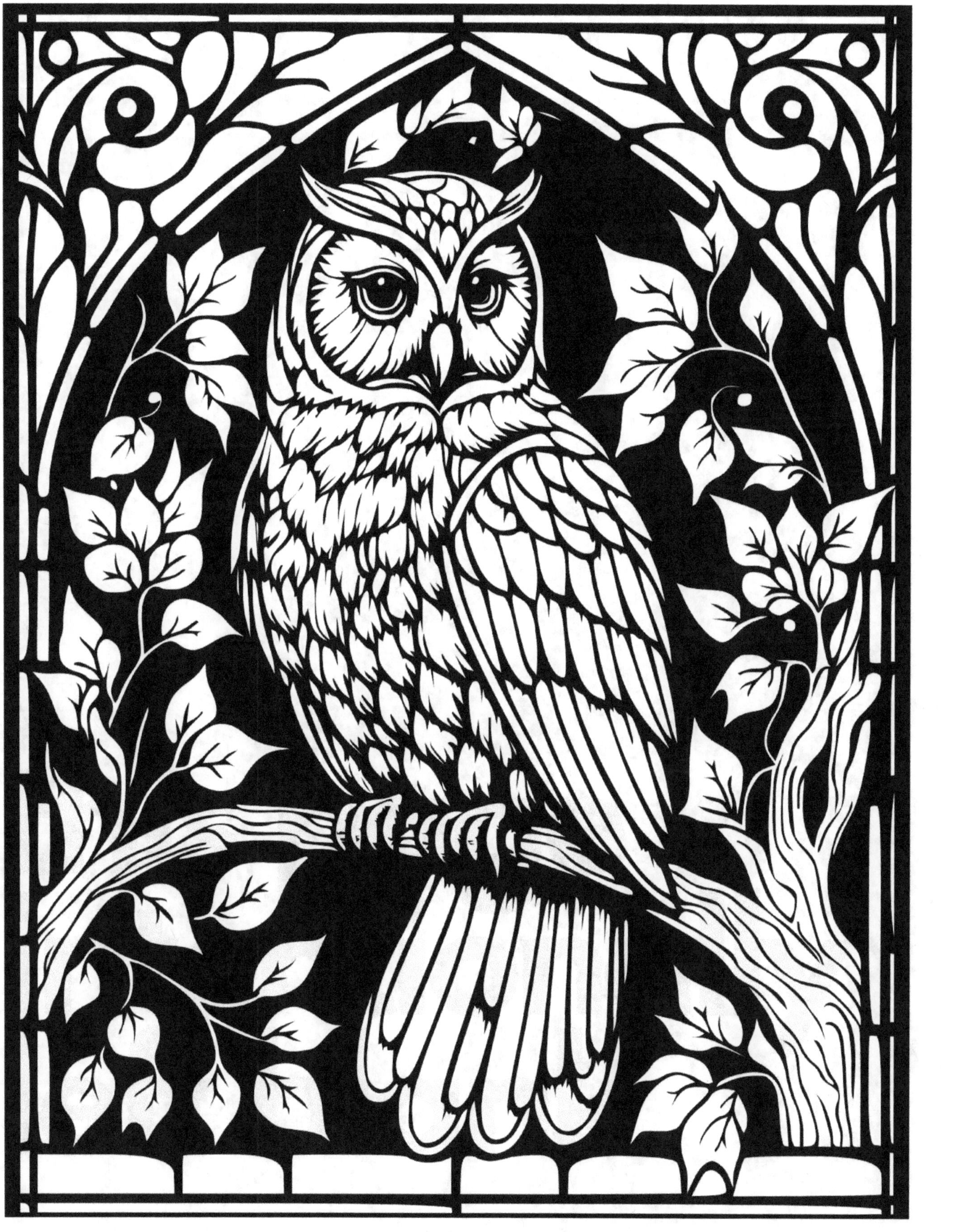

this page intentionally left blank

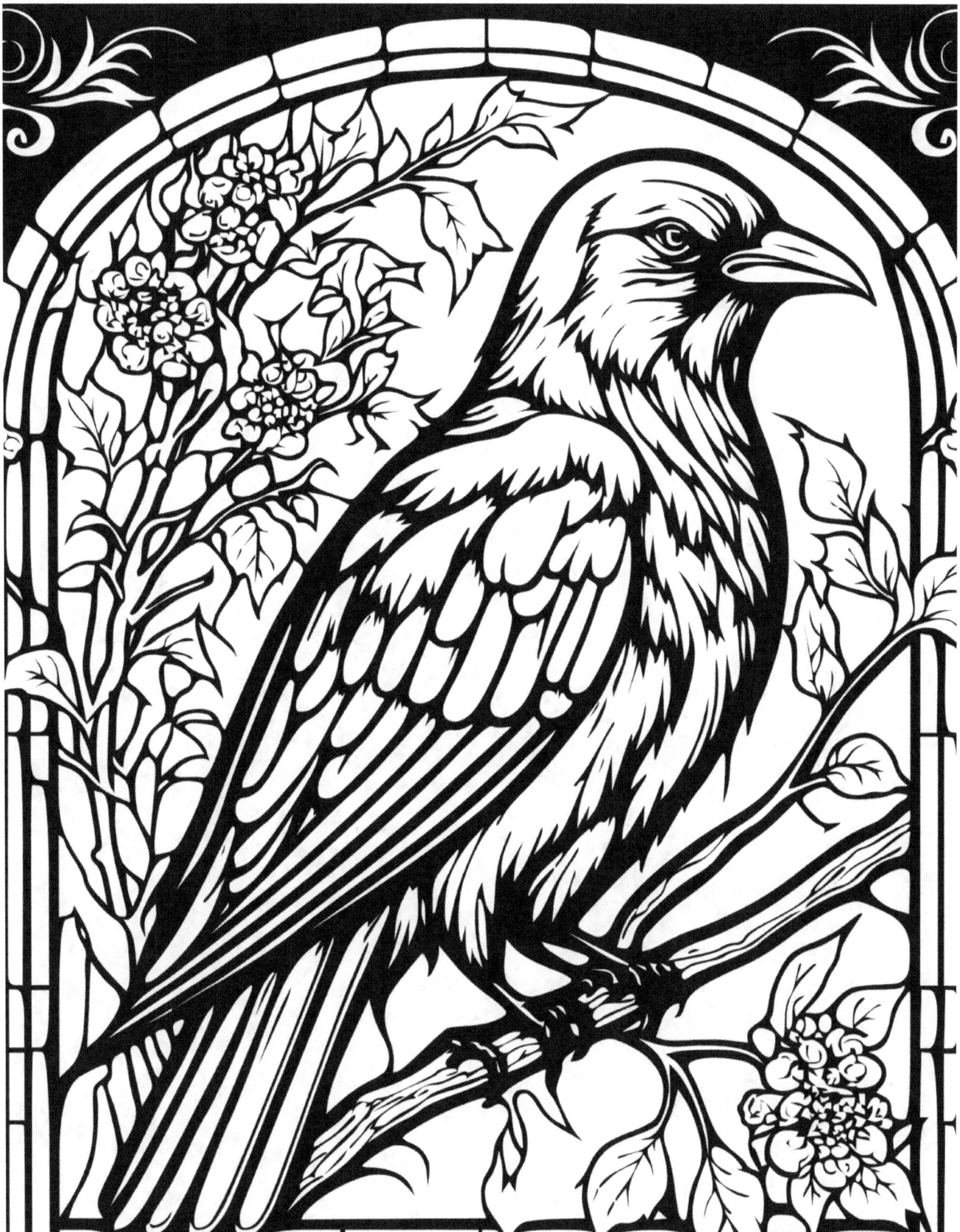

this page intentionally left blank

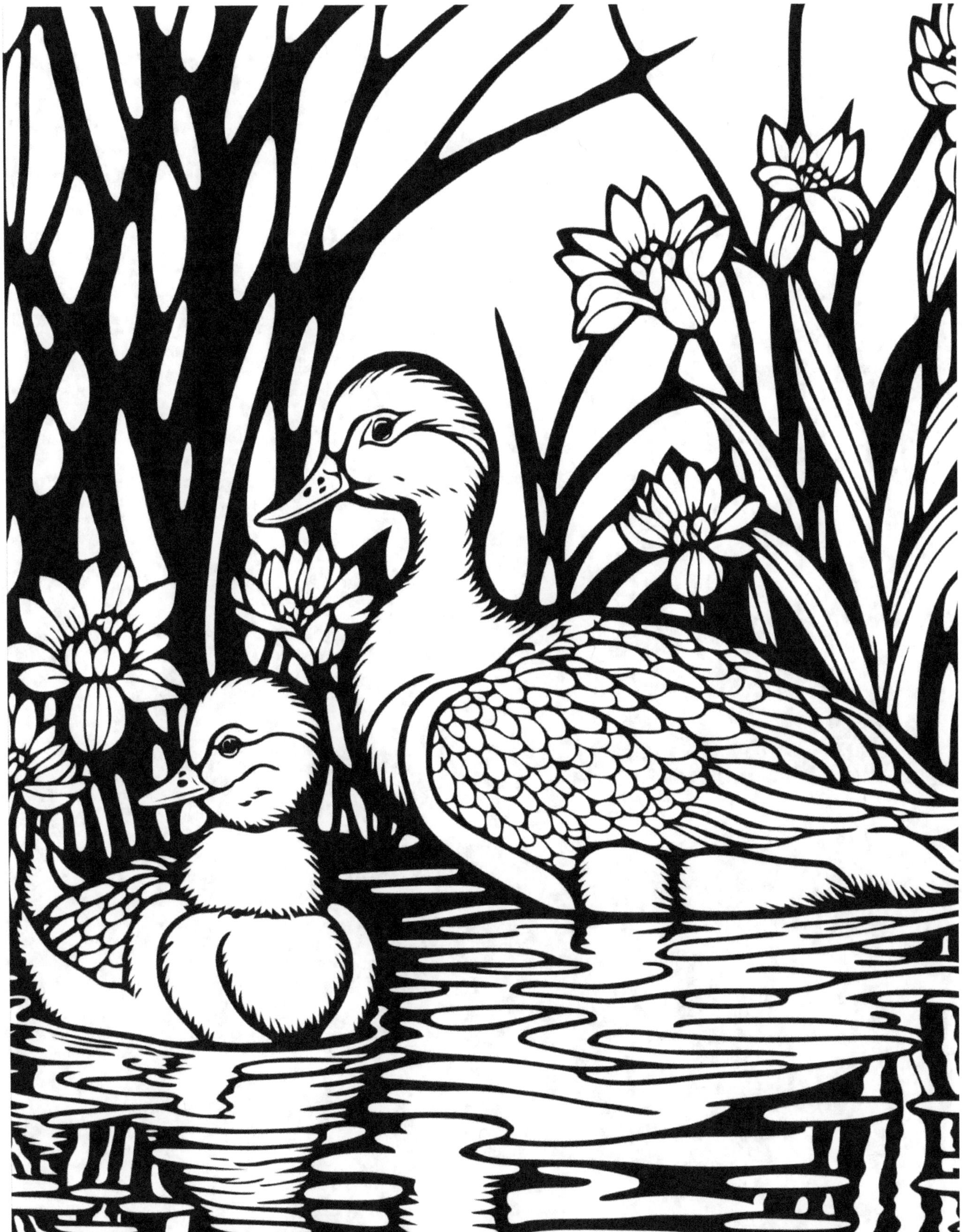

this page intentionally left blank

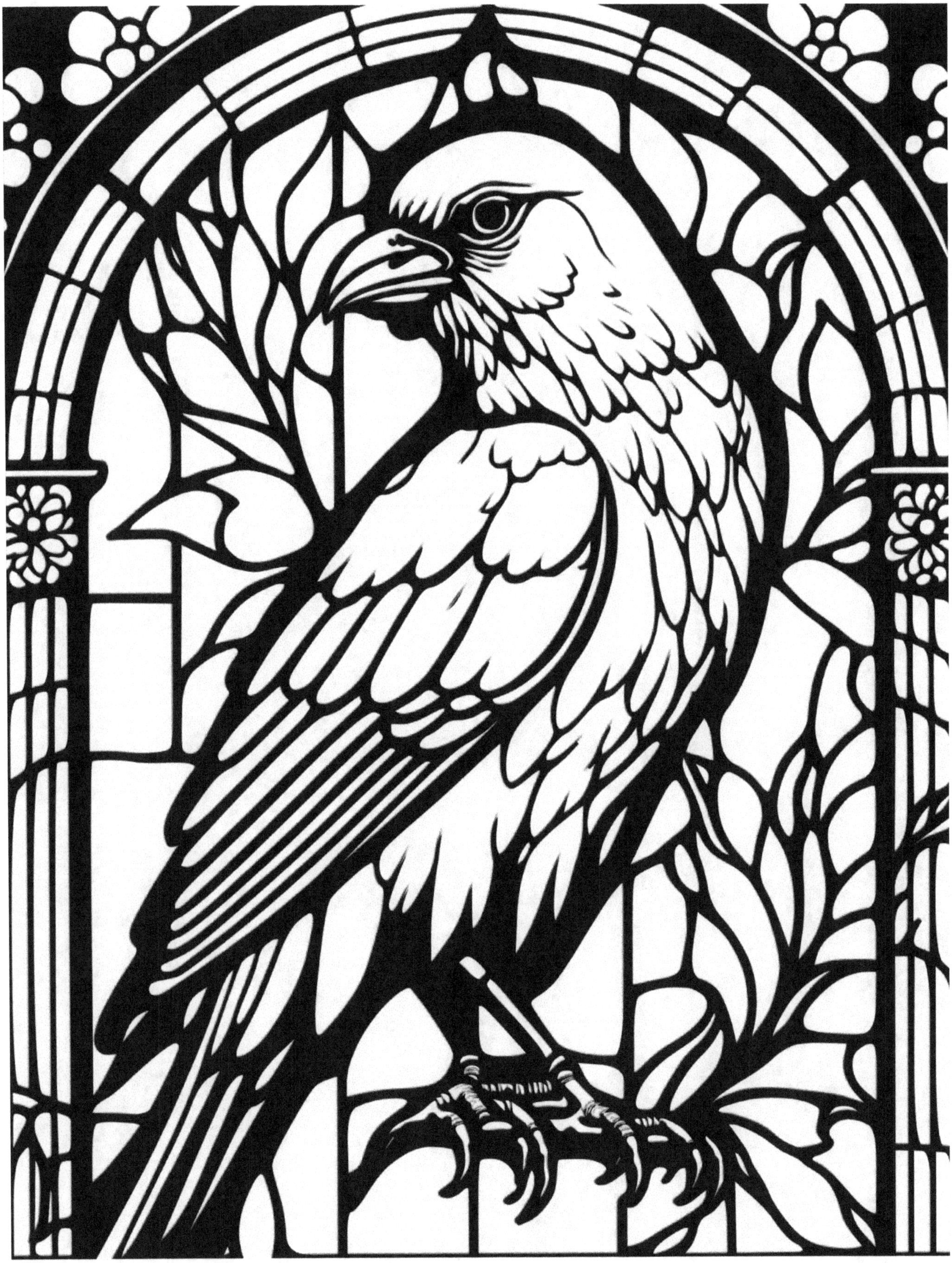

this page intentionally left blank

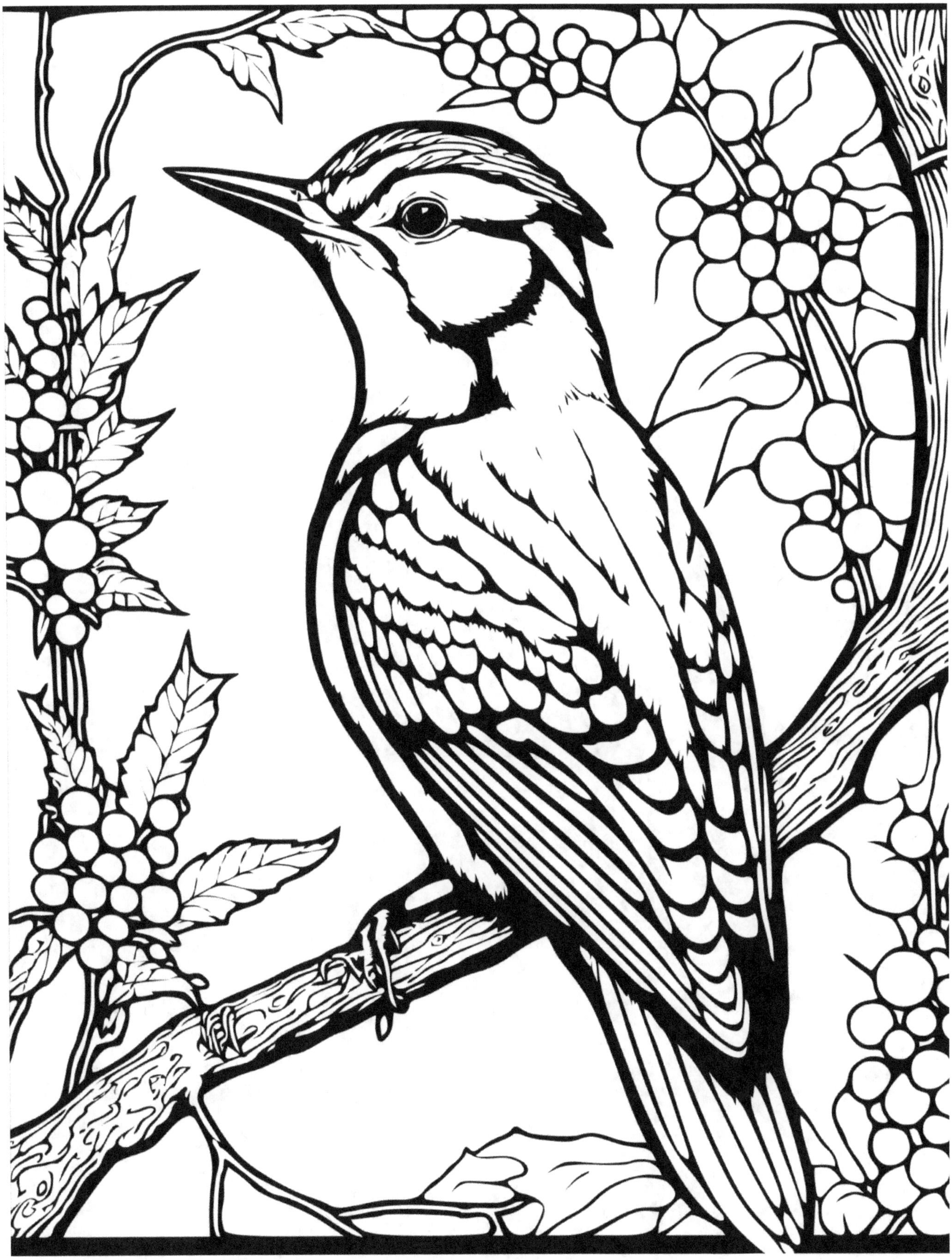

this page intentionally left blank

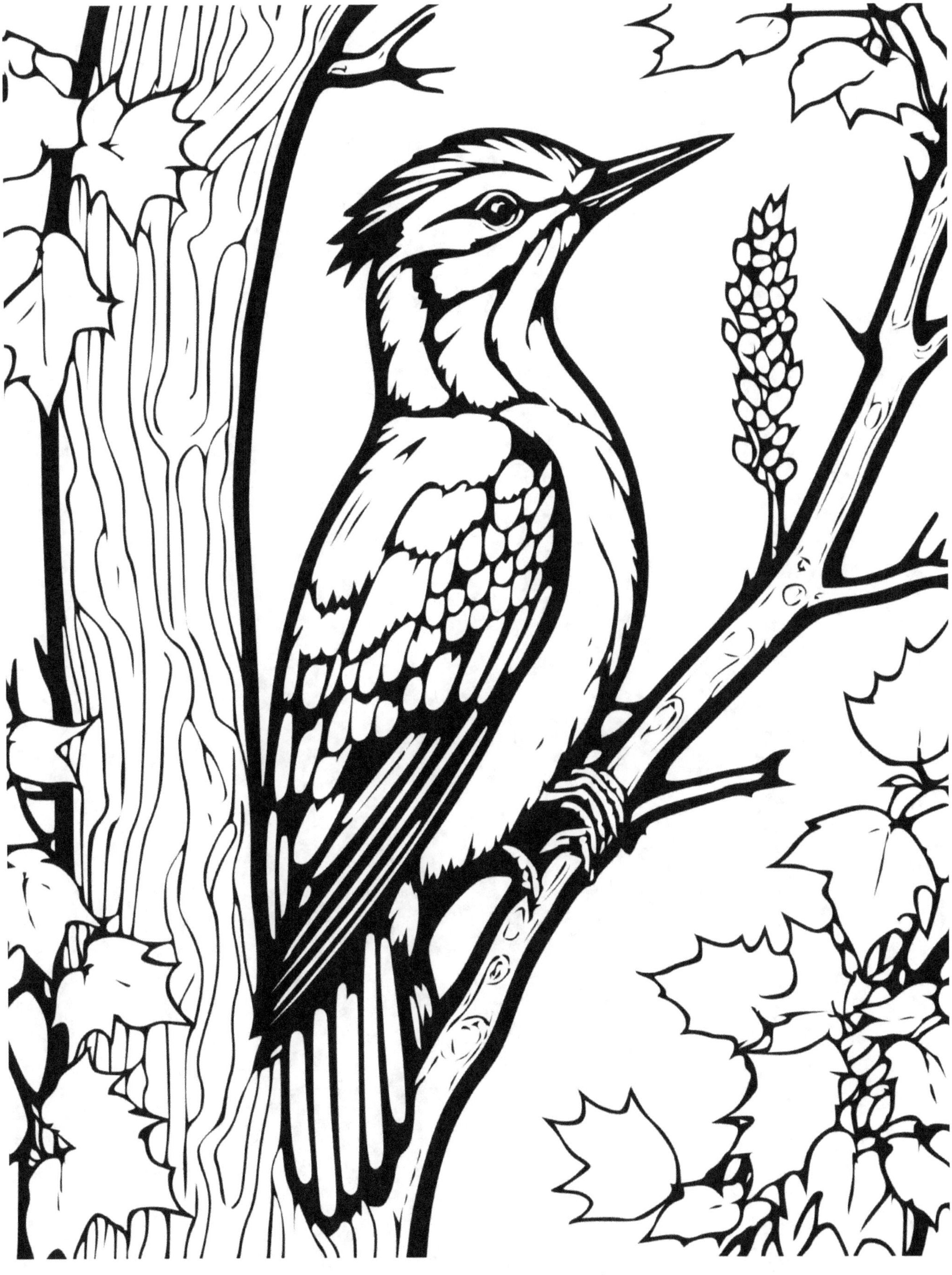

this page intentionally left blank

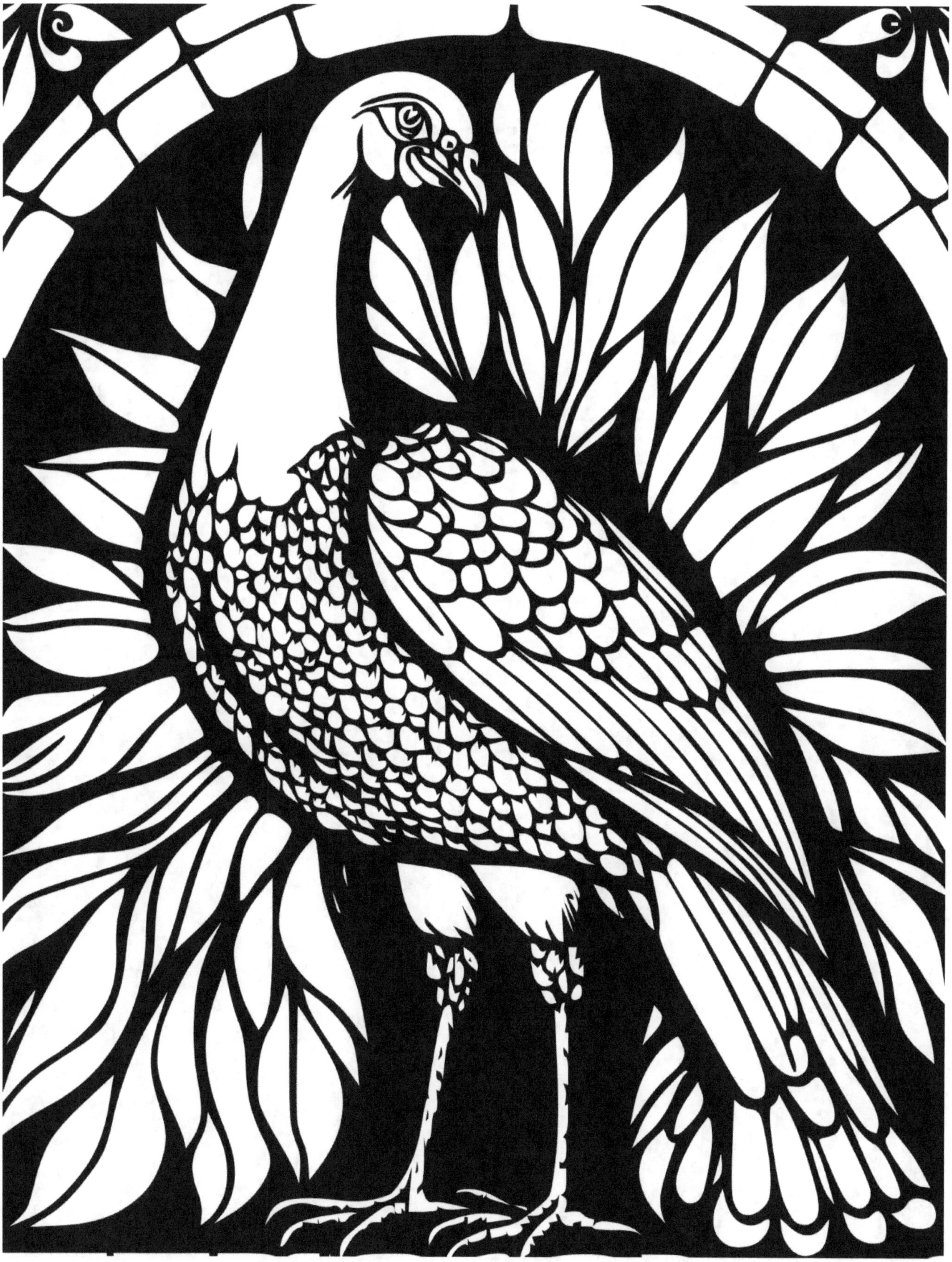

this page intentionally left blank

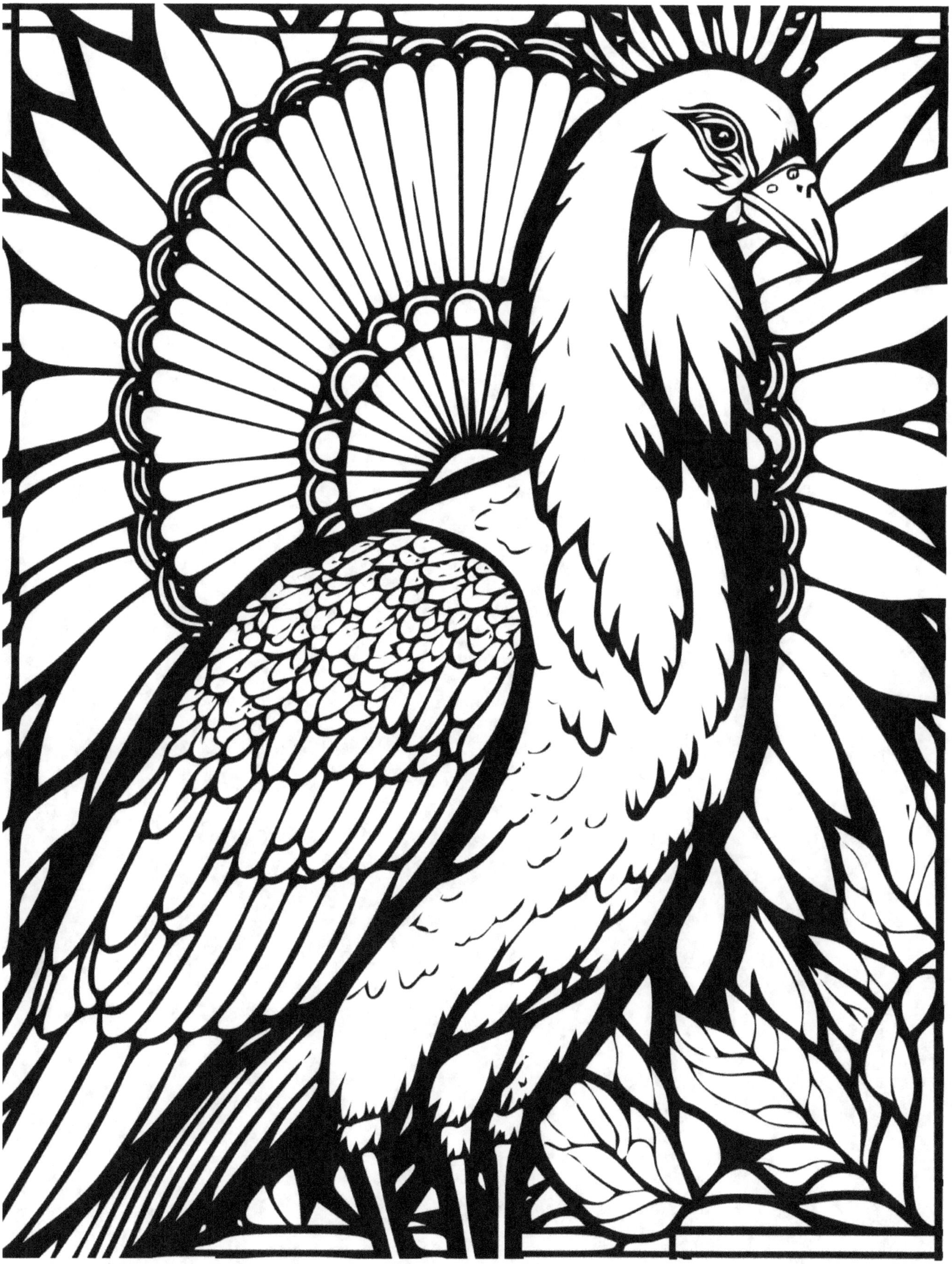

this page intentionally left blank

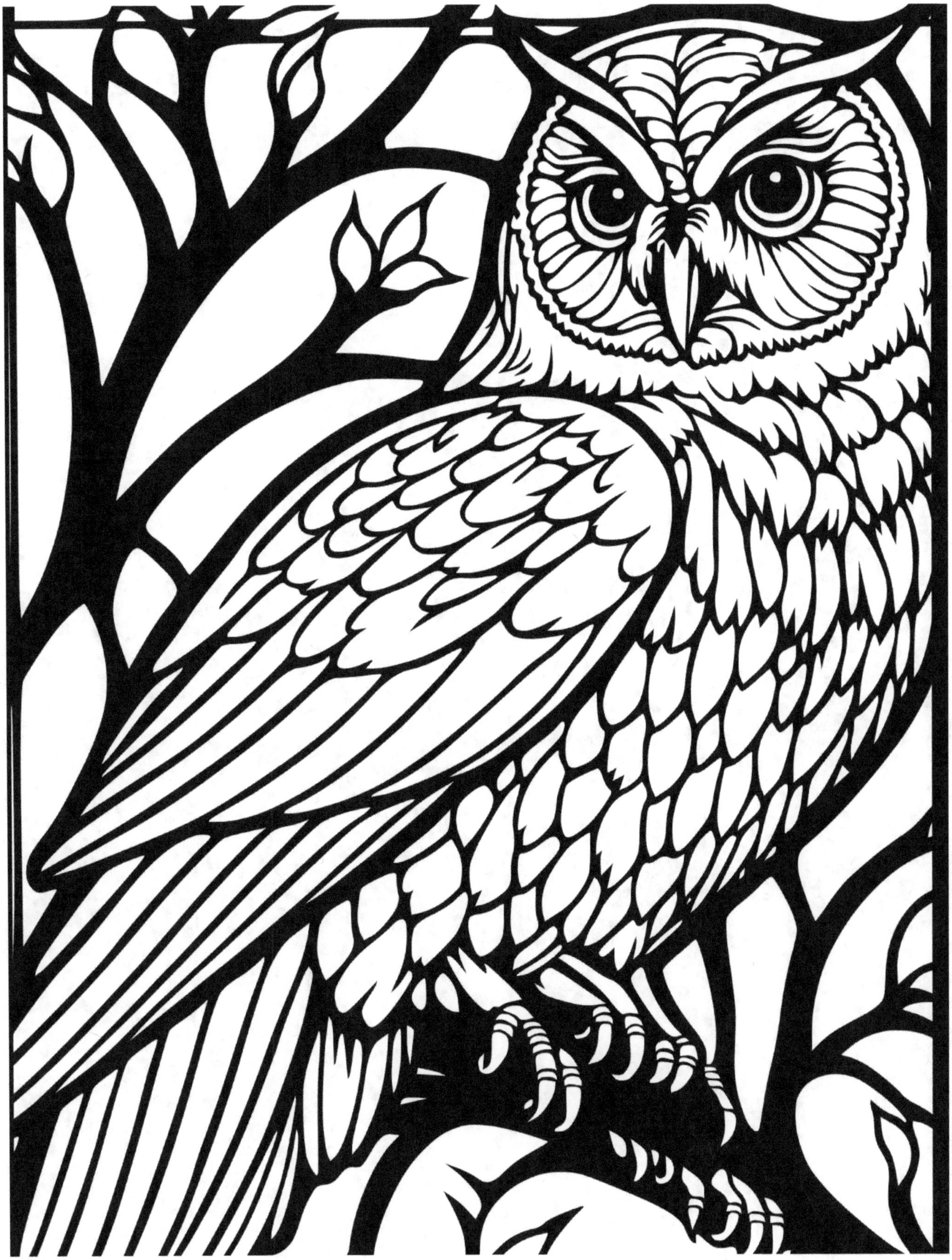

this page intentionally left blank

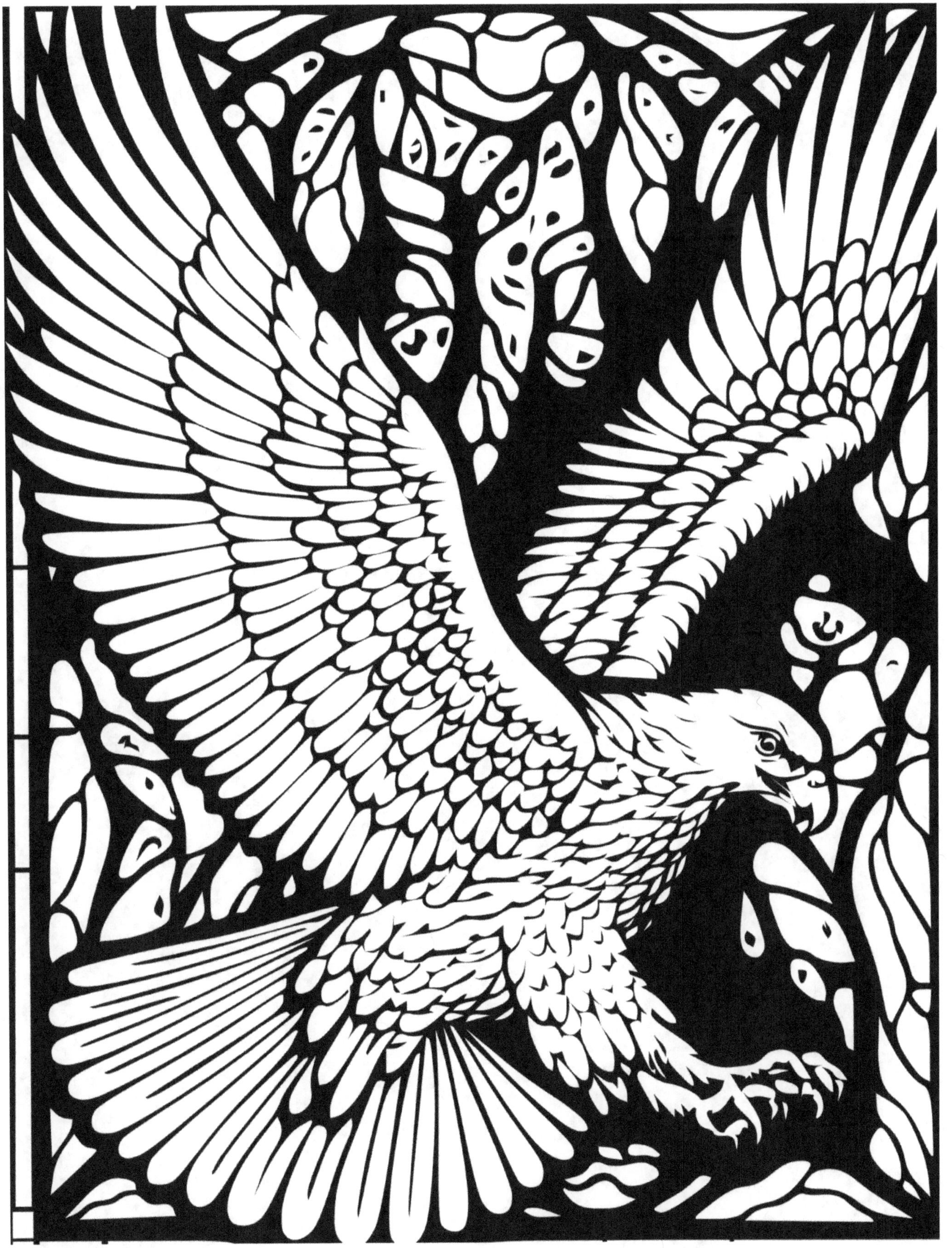

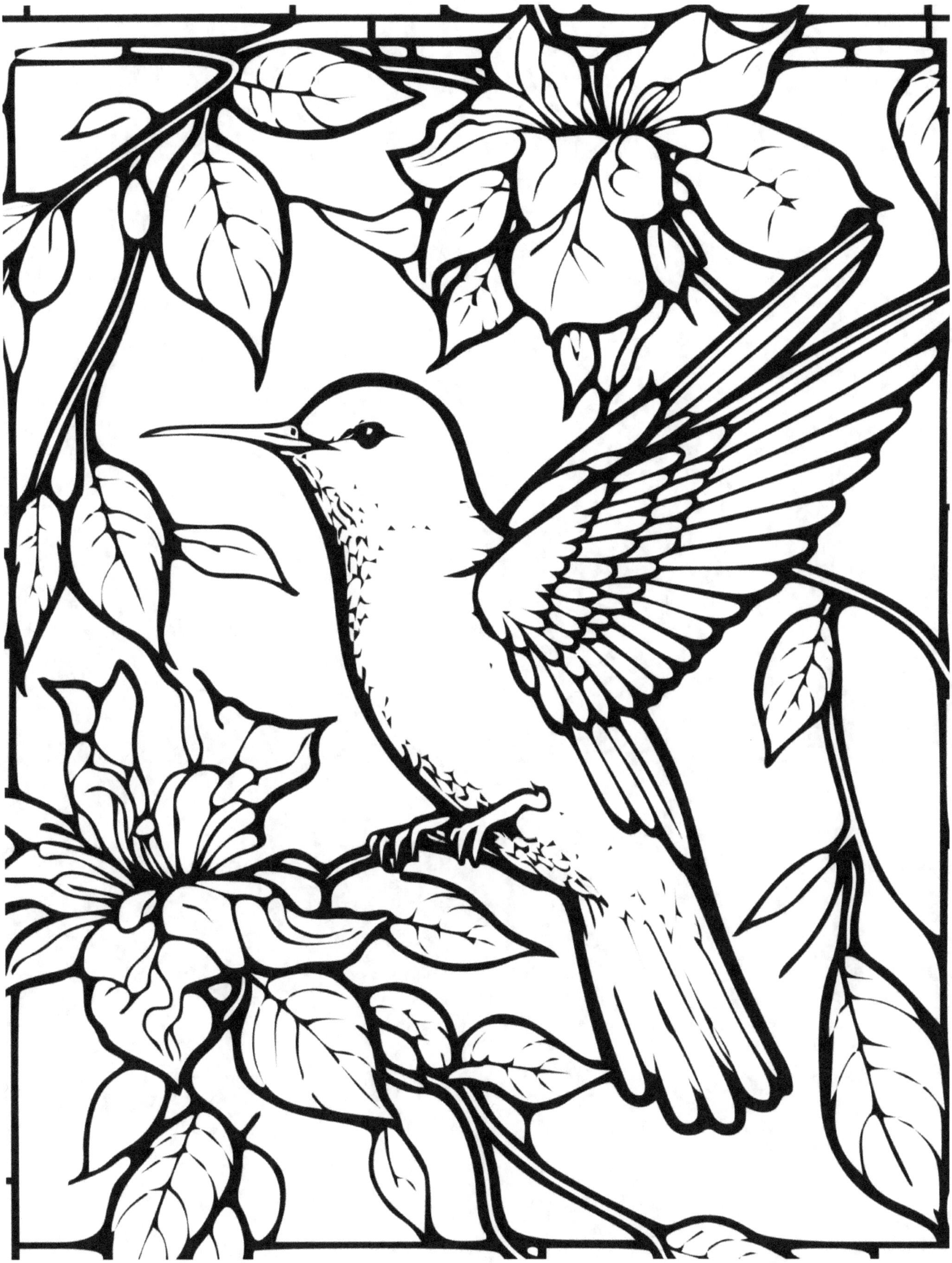

this page intentionally left blank

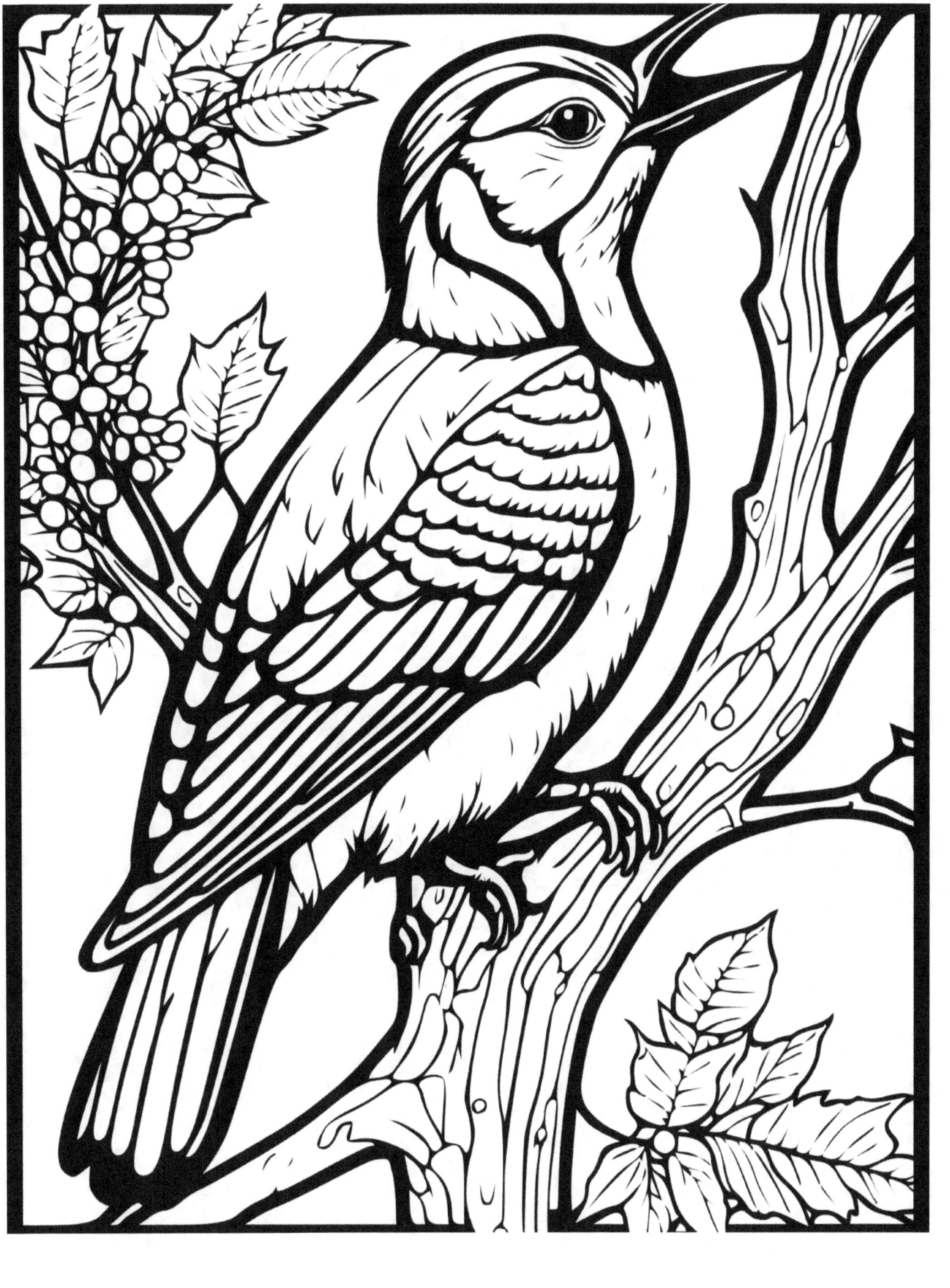

this page intentionally left blank

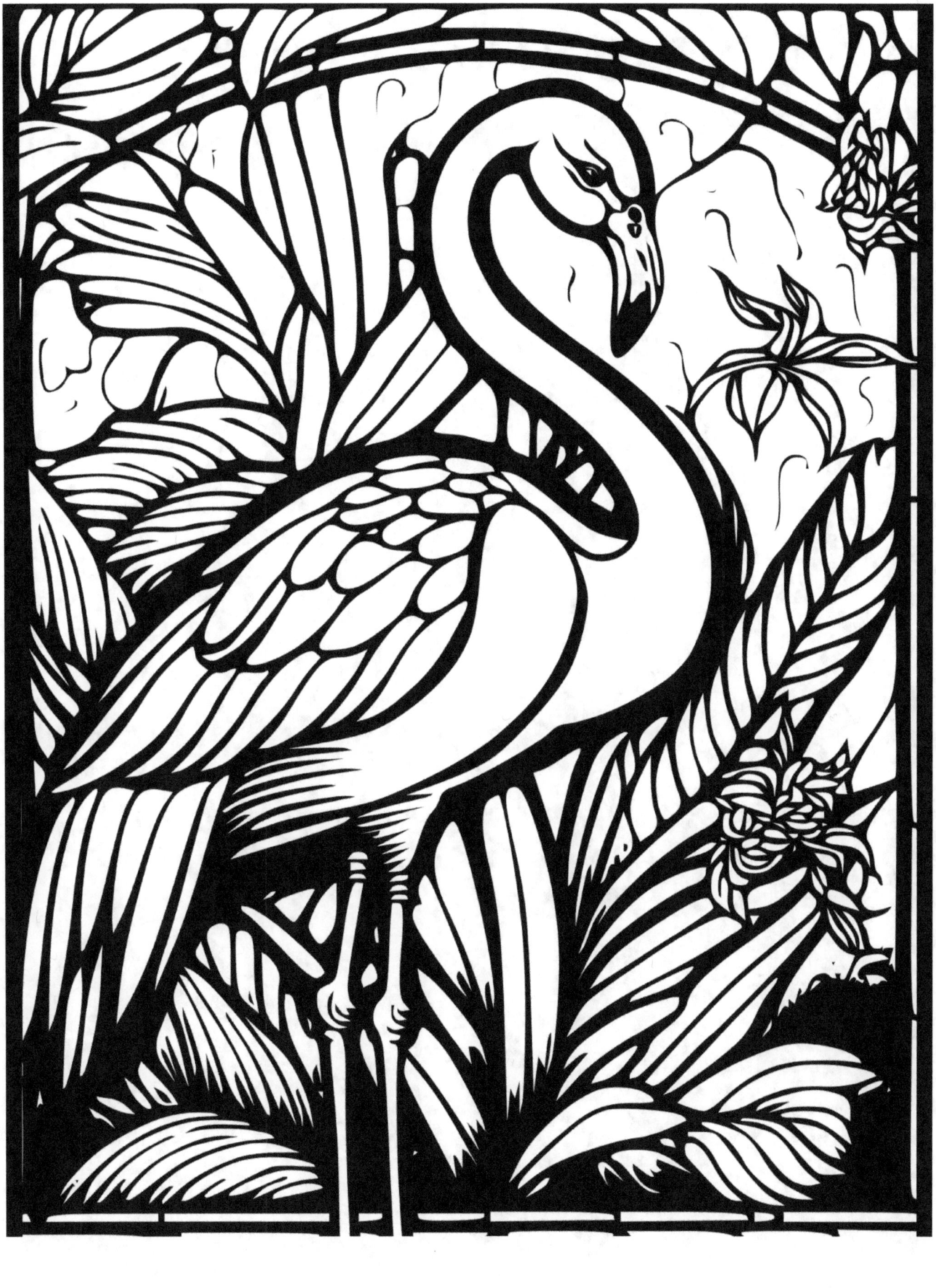

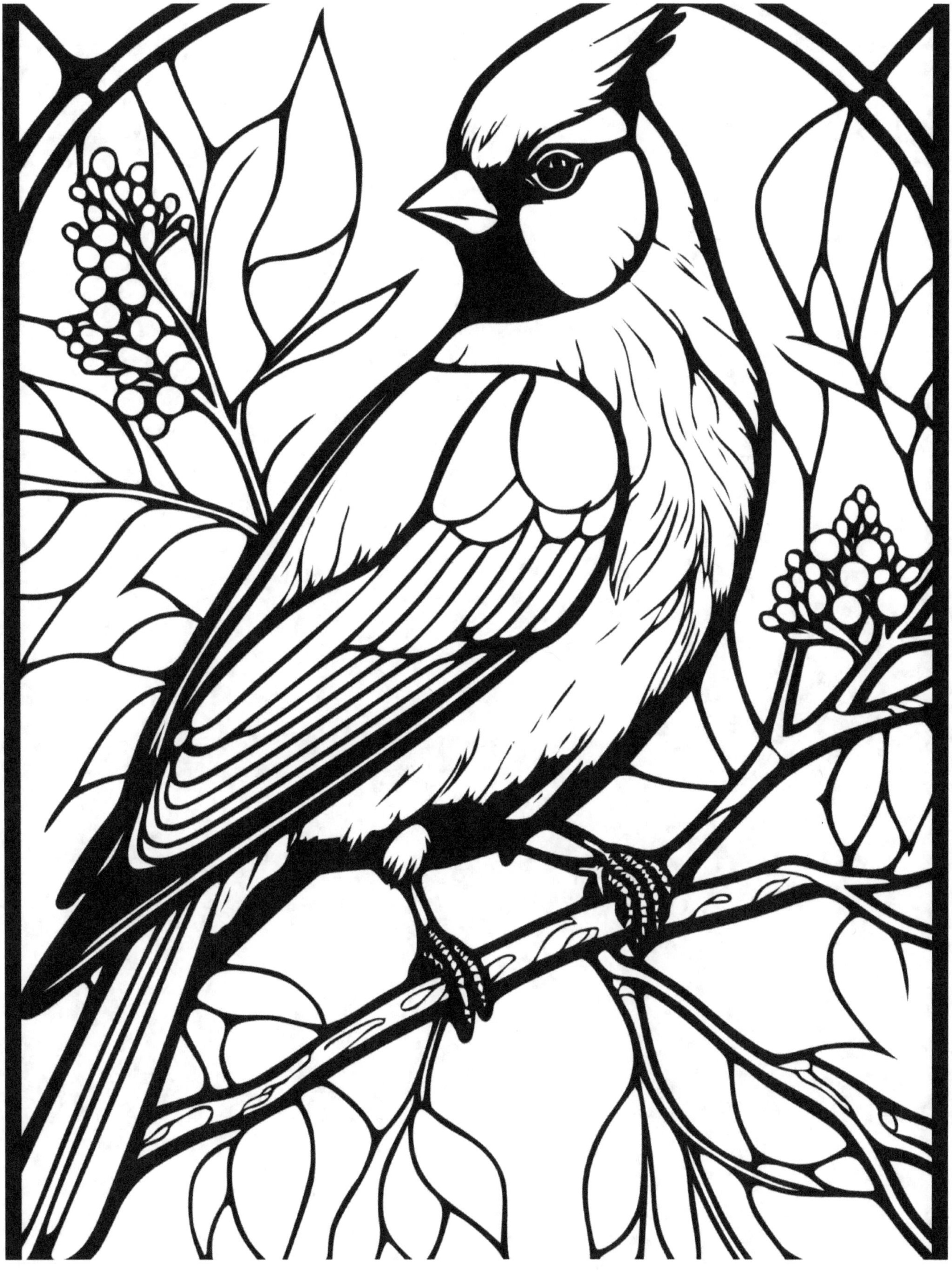

this page intentionally left blank

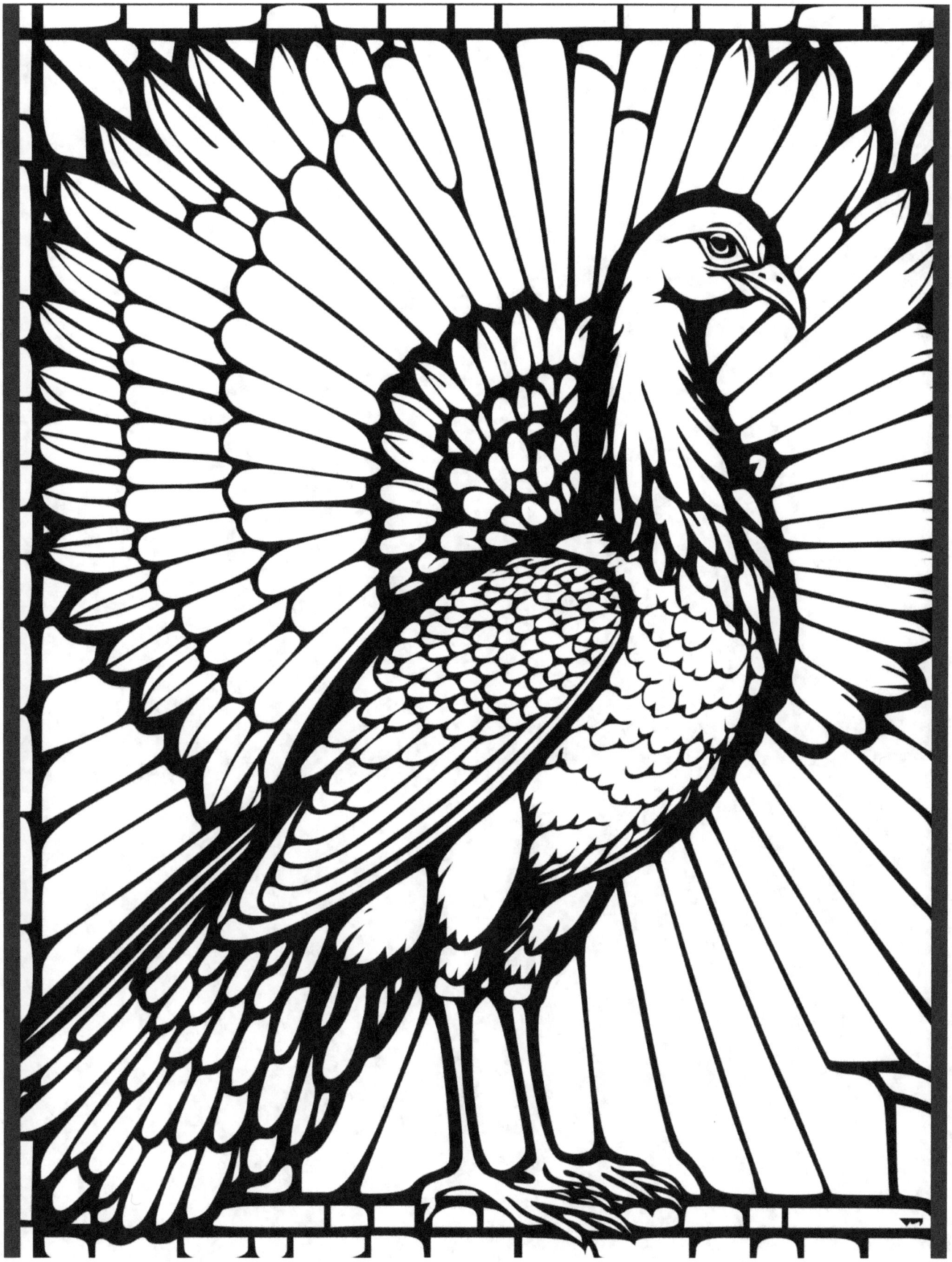

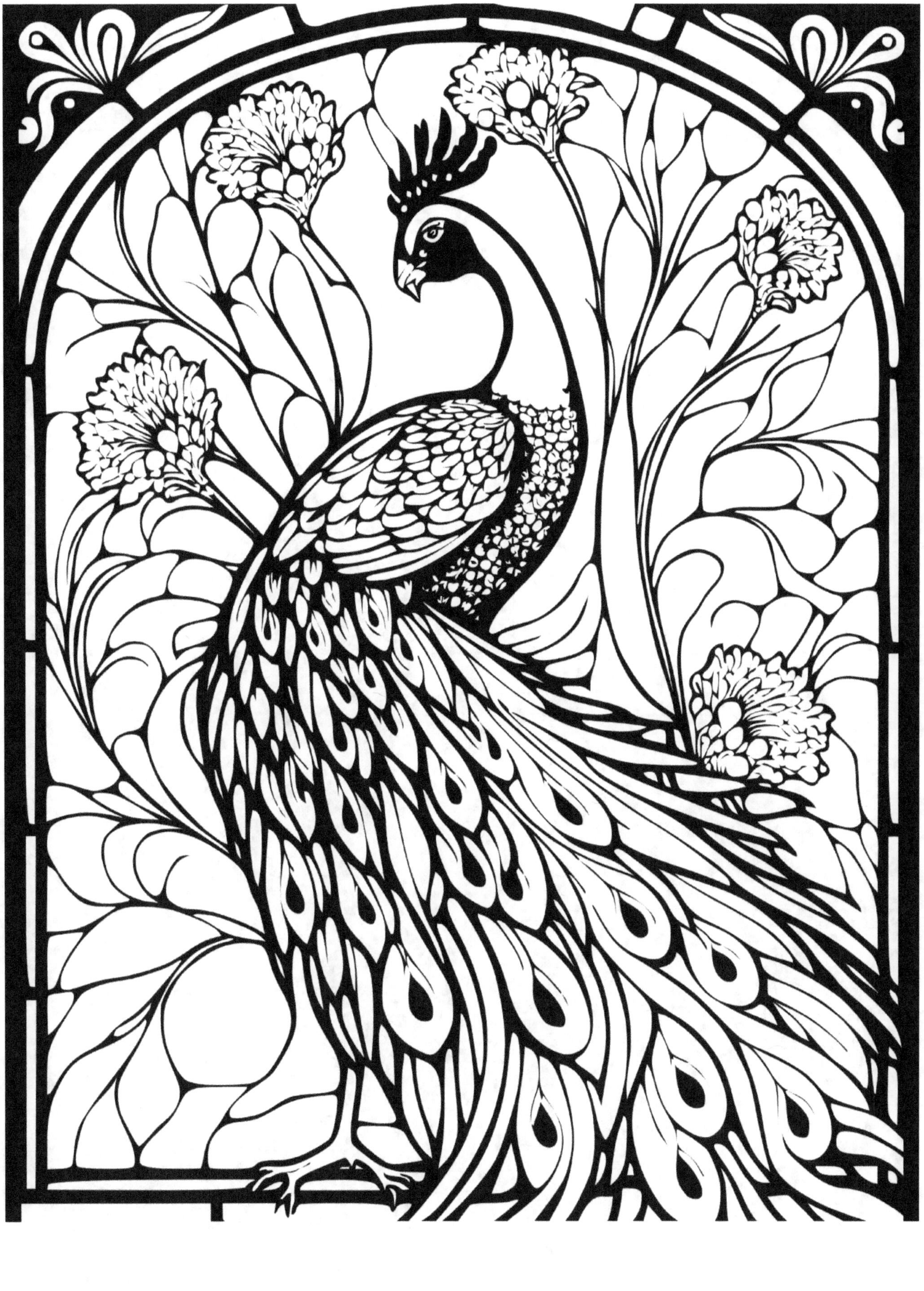

this page intentionally left blank

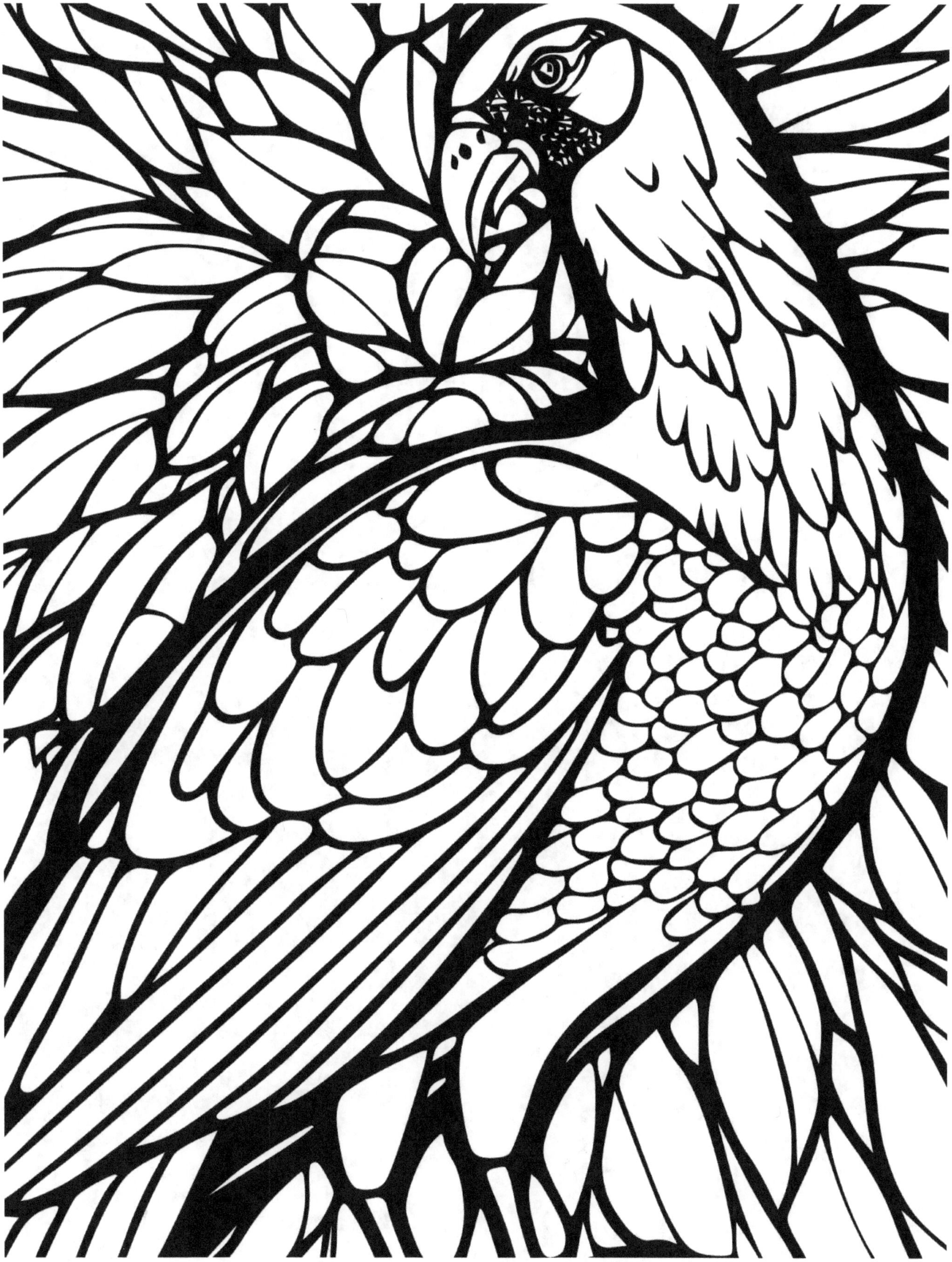

this page intentionally left blank

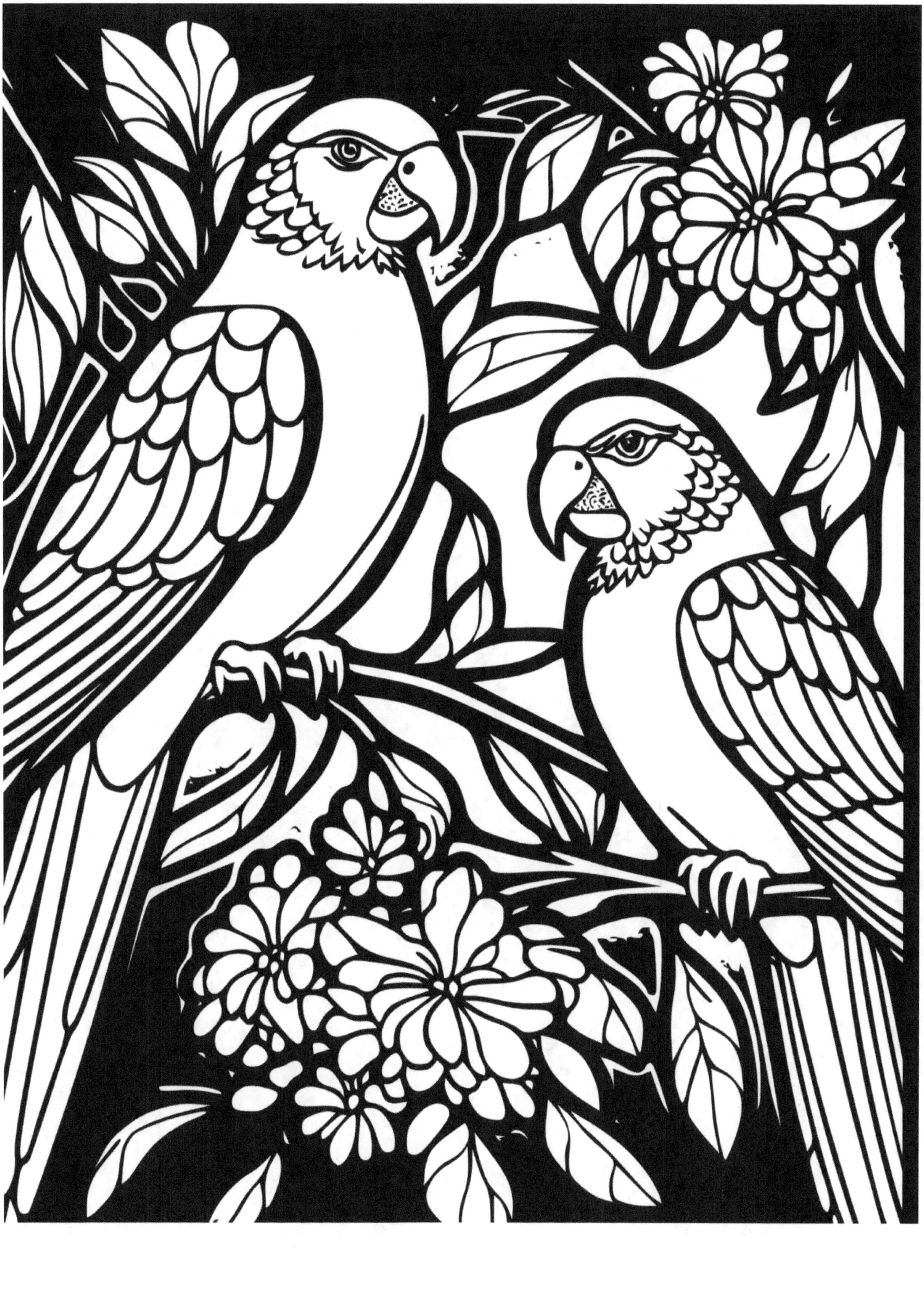

this page intentionally left blank

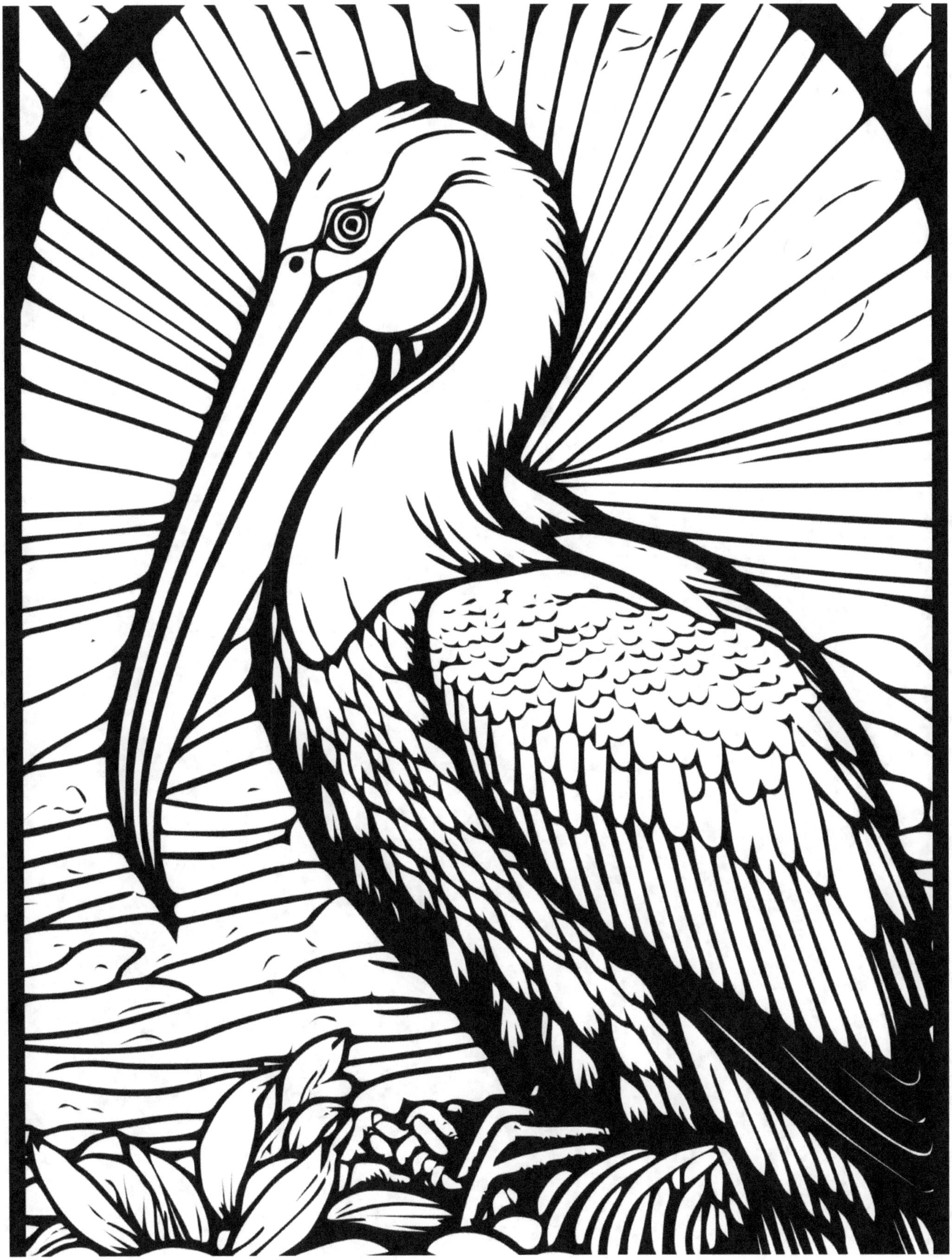

this page intentionally left blank

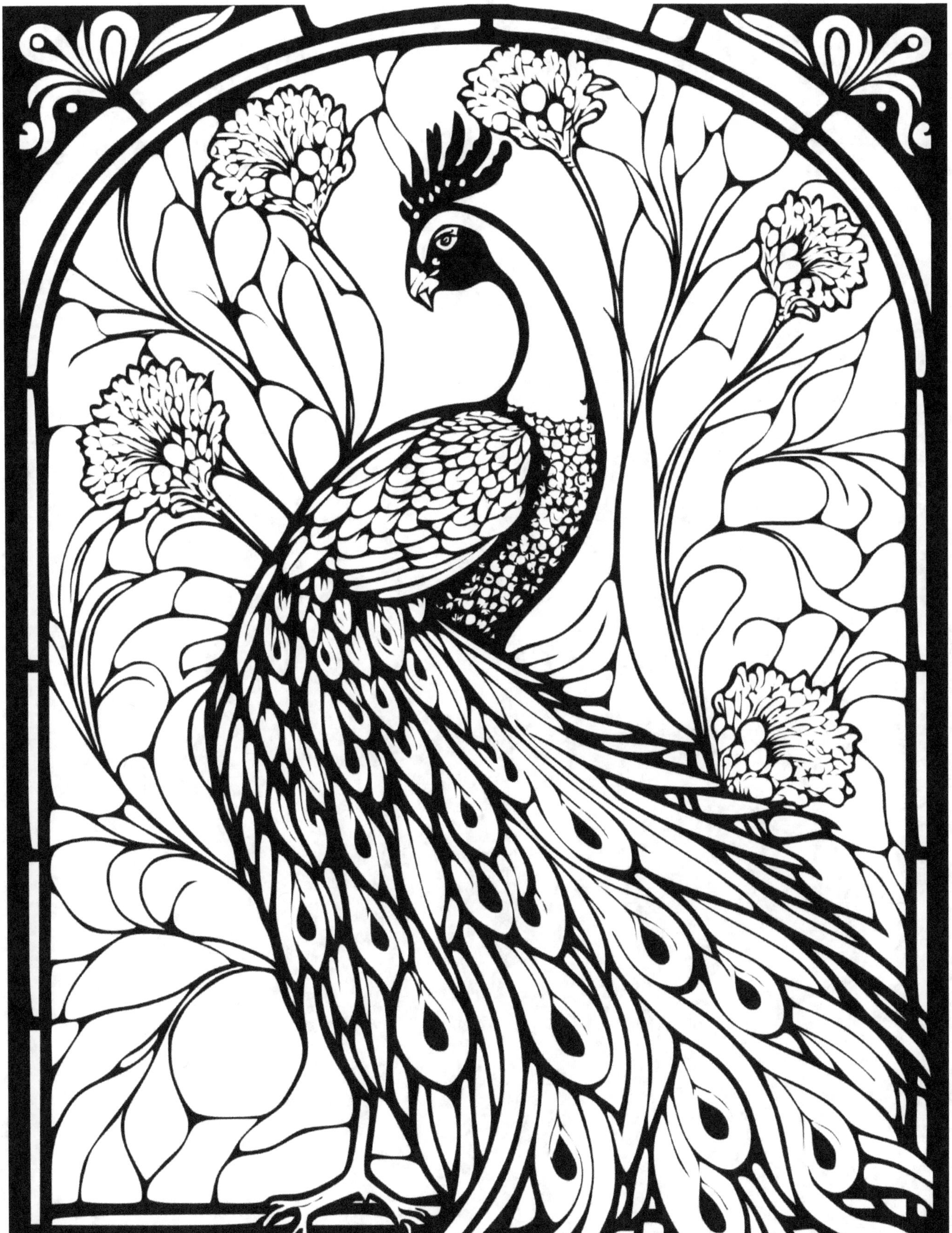

www.ingramcontent.com/pod-product-compliance
Lightning Source LLC
Chambersburg PA
CBHW081059240526
45465CB00025B/2774
* 9 7 9 8 3 7 4 5 8 4 2 1 9 *